David McLellan was born in Hertford in 1940, and was educated at Merchant Taylors' School and St John's College, Oxford. He has been Visiting Professor at the State University of New York and Guest Fellow in Politics in the Indian Institute of Advanced Study, Simla, India. He is currently Professor of Political Theory at the University of Kent. He has lectured widely in North America and on the Continent of Europe and his publications (which have been translated into many languages) include *The Young Hegelians and Karl Marx* (1969), *Marx before Marxism* (1970), *Karl Marx: The Early Texts* (1971), *Marx's Grundrisse* (1971), *The Thought of Karl Marx* (1971), and *Karl Marx: His Life and Thought* (1973). He is also the author of the Modern Masters volume, *Marx* (1975).

D1003033

Modern Masters

ARTAUD	Martin Esslin
BECKETT	A. Alvarez
CAMUS	Conor Cruise O'Brien
CHOMSKY	John Lyons
EINSTEIN	Jeremy Bernstein
ELIOT	Stephen Spender
FANON	David Caute
FREUD	Richard Wollheim
GANDHI	George Woodcock
GRAMSCI	James Joll
JOYCE	John Gross
JUNG	Anthony Storr
KAFKA	Erich Heller
KEYNES	D. E. Moggridge
LAING	Edgar Z. Friedenberg
LAWRENCE	Frank Kermode
LE CORBUSIER	Stephen Gardiner
LENIN	Robert Conquest
LÉVI-STRAUSS	Edmund Leach
LUKÁCS	George Lichtheim
MARCUSE	Alasdair MacIntyre
MARX	David McLellan
MCLUHAN	Jonathan Miller
ORWELL	Raymond Williams
POPPER	Bryan Magee
POUND	Donald Davie
PROUST	Roger Shattuck
REICH	Charles Rycroft
RUSSELL	A. J. Ayer
SARTRE	Arthur C. Danto
SAUSSURE	Jonathan Culler
SCHOENBERG	Charles Rosen
WEBER	Donald MacRae
WITTGENSTEIN	David Pears
YEATS	Denis Donoghue

To be followed by
BARTHES	Annette Lavers
DURKHEIM	Anthony Giddens
EVANS-PRITCHARD	Mary Douglas
KLEIN	Hanna Segal
JAKOBSON	Thomas A. Sebeok
MERLEAU-PONTY	Herbert Dreyfus
NIETZSCHE	J. P. Stern
PAVLOV	J. A. Gray
TROTSKY	Irving Howe

Engels

David McLellan

Fontana/Collins

First published in Fontana 1977

Copyright © David McLellan 1977

Made and printed in Great Britain by
William Collins Sons and Co. Ltd, Glasgow

To Gabrielle and Stephanie

Contents

Preface   9

1 Life   11

2 History   27

3 Politics   42

4 Philosophy   56

5 Conclusion: Engels and Marx   65

Further Reading   76

Chronology   78

Preface

The following is an attempt to give a brief description of Engels' life and thought. The book begins with a biographical sketch, continues with chapters on various aspects of Engels' thought and finishes with a conclusion that aims to delineate (largely through a contrast with Marx) Engels' original contribution to the Marxist tradition. It is in this last area that Engels is most clearly a Modern Master. It is true that he did pioneering work of a sort in such disparate fields as anthropology, urban sociology, and guerrilla tactics; but his chief claim to influence in the modern world is that it was Engels who gave decisive shape to the world-view that came to be known as dialectical materialism. The millions who have given their allegiance to orthodox communism have been indebted primarily to Engels for their understanding of communist doctrine – at least in the fields of history and philosophy.

I am grateful to my friends Gay Sharp and Graham Thomas for reading parts of the manuscript and much improving its style.

13 Ivy Lane, Canterbury
January 1977

1 Life

Nothing in Engels' ancestry or upbringing foreshadowed the future revolutionary. A prosperous business family, a strongly religious ethos, and a contempt for learning (which did not even allow Engels to finish his schooling) do not seem fertile ground for the breeding of socialist intellectuals. The fortunes of the family that was, according to one of its traditions, of Huguenot origin (named D'Ange) had been securely established by Engels' great-grandfather, Johann Caspar Engels. He created a bleaching and spinning works in Barmen near Düsseldorf in the Rhineland. Engels' father took his share of the business into a partnership with the brothers Godfrey and Peter Ermen to form a prosperous enterprise with factories both in Barmen and in Manchester. His wife, a much gentler, more sensitive and humorous person than he, came from a family of Dutch schoolteachers. Their son Friedrich, born on 28 November 1820, was the eldest of a family of eight.

Barmen is situated in the most industrialized area of Germany – it was known as 'little Manchester' – and afforded constant evidence of the progress and effects of the Industrial Revolution. It was also a centre of a strict Pietism which flourished in the early nineteenth century as a reaction against the rationalism of the French Revolution. Like the English Puritans, the Pietists held to the literal truth of the Bible, were intolerant of differing views, and frowned on the pursuit of worldly pleasures. The enthusiasm of Engels' father for business was only matched by his attachment to the church, and young Friedrich's early life was shaped by his struggle against both.

During his last years of school, Engels had decided to devote his life to literature, but his father insisted that he enter the family business in Barmen – which he did at the early age of sixteen and spent a year learning its rudiments and writing poetry in his spare time. In 1838 his father sent Engels to continue his businessman's apprenticeship in the Hanseatic port of Bremen. Here Engels began to enjoy experiences previously impossible within the narrow confines of Barmen. In the office of Consul Leupold, where he helped as an unsalaried clerk, work was not strictly supervised and there was plenty of free time for beer drinking and reading during office hours. Engels was given a key to his lodgings and enjoyed to the full the cosmopolitan social life of Bremen. He wrote to one of his friends: 'To get the most out of life you must be active, you must live, and you must have the courage to taste the thrill of being young.' His reading was voracious and wide. In particular his views on religion began to evolve under the influence of Strauss and Schleimacher, radical theologians who attacked the dogmatic foundations of orthodox Christianity: 'I have come to the conclusion,' he wrote, 'only to treat a teaching as divine if it can defend itself before the bar of reason.' His developing views were expressed in the articles that he began to get published while in Bremen. These consisted mainly of vivid descriptions of social life in Bremen, but included a series with some biting criticism of social conditions in the Wupper valley. Engels declared himself a disciple of the Young German Movement, a literary movement whose members (the most prominent being the poet Heinrich Heine) were radical in politics, very liberal in religion, and had a marked interest in social questions. But Engels soon found his chosen career of literature insufficiently satisfying and turned to philosophy.

At that time Berlin was Germany's leading university and the centre of the radical Hegelianism that Engels was beginning to find so attractive. He was therefore glad to leave Bremen in April 1841 and, after six months at home, to go and do his military service in Berlin, as a one-year volunteer in the Guards Foot Artillery. He immediately joined the company of the Young Hegelians – a group of young intellectuals who wished to use Hegel's ideas, particularly those of dialectic and negativity, to develop a critique of contemporary religion and politics. Hegel had viewed history as the progress of Spirit in which each historical epoch and its attendant ideas was only a passing stage, due to be negated and transcended dialectically by the next stage. The Young Hegelians wished to explore the way in which the religious and political ideas of their own age were destined to give rise to a more satisfactory view of the world. As Engels himself wrote later:

> The doctrine of Hegel, taken as a whole, left plenty of room for giving shelter to the most diverse practical party views. And in the theoretical Germany of that time two things above all were practical: religion and politics. Whoever placed chief emphasis on the Hegelian *system* could be fairly conservative in both spheres; whoever regarded the dialectical *method* as the main thing could belong to the most extreme opposition, both in politics and religion.

Engels arrived in Berlin at the brief flowering of the Young Hegelian Movement. Following the accession of Frederick William IV censorship restrictions were briefly lifted, and Ludwig Feuerbach had just published his *Essence of Christianity* which claimed to show that religion was merely the projection on to God of man's innate desires and capacities – a thesis whose combination of materialism and humanism aroused widespread enthusiasm among his fellow Young Hegelians. According to Engels, 'we all became Feuerbachians'. Engels' arrival in Berlin also co-incided with the much-heralded course of inaugural lectures by the old Schelling, who had been a friend and colleague of Hegel's in his youth but was now recalled to Berlin by the government to stem the tide of radical Hegelianism. Engels attacked Schelling's rather mystical defence of orthodox Christianity in two anonymous pamphlets which marked his final break with the religion of his youth. By their vigorous defence of Hegelianism and contempt for orthodox religion they attracted widespread attention and curiosity about the author – who was at first thought to be Bakunin.

On terminating his military service in October 1842 Engels went to Cologne on a trip that gave his life its definitive orientation. His immediate purpose in stopping in Cologne on his way home was to meet the editors of the *Rheinische Zeitung* – a radical newspaper, founded by Rhenish industrialists to propagate their liberal doctrines, which had opened its columns to the Berlin Young Hegelians. The moving spirit behind the paper – at least in its inception – was Moses Hess, known as 'the Communist rabbi'. Like Engels, he came from a prosperous business family and had educated himself towards communism. In a series of books written in a meandering style and almost Messianic tone, Hess had been the first of the Young Hegelians to proclaim a version of communism. Strongly influenced by French sociology and particularly the Utopian socialism of Saint-Simon with its positive emphasis on the development of industry, Hess turned Hegel's philosophy towards the future and asserted that Feuerbach's philosophical humanism and the French notions of class struggle were about to be put into practice through a communist revolution in the most economically-advanced country – England.

These ideas had a profound effect on Engels. Hess wrote concerning their meeting: 'We talked of questions of the day. Engels, who was revolutionary to the core when he met me, left as a passionate Communist.' He therefore decided to unite his business career and political interest by going to work for a spell in his father's factory in Manchester, situated in the industrial heartland of the country of the future. On his way there he stopped off again in Cologne – and this time met the youthful editor of the *Rheinische Zeitung* – Karl Marx. The meeting was a cool one. Marx saw in Engels merely a representative of the Berlin Young Hegelians with whom he was on the point of breaking since they considered the paper to be, according to Marx, 'above all a vehicle for theological propaganda, atheism, etc., instead of political discussion and action'. Engels, however, continued to write for the *Rheinische Zeitung*, in the manner wished for by Marx, on his arrival in England.

Engels' stay in Manchester from 1842 to 1844 was decisive for his intellectual development. 'In Manchester', he wrote later,

> it was forcibly brought to my notice that economic factors, hitherto ignored or at least underestimated by historians, play a decisive role in the development of the modern world. I learnt that economic factors were the basic cause of the clash between different classes in society. And I realized that in a highly industrialized country like England the clash of social classes lay at the very root of the rivalry between parties and was of fundamental significance in tracing the course of modern political history.

While in Manchester, Engels continued his correspondence for German papers and in particular sent two articles to the *Deutsch-Französische Jahrbücher* which Marx was edit-ing in Paris, following the suppression of the *Rheinische Zeitung*. One of these, entitled *Outlines of a Critique of Political Economy*, proclaimed in stark and simple language the idea of the inevitable impoverishment of the working class and consequent revolution. It directed Marx's atten-tion to the subject of economics. Thus, when Engels passed through Paris in September 1844 on his way back to the Rhineland, he and Marx had an entirely different encounter from that of the previous year: 'When I visited Marx in Paris in the summer of 1844 we found ourselves in com-plete agreement on questions of theory and our collabora-tion began at that time.'

Engels' most immediate task on returning to Barmen was to write up the material he had gathered in Manchester into his classic indictment of early British capitalism — *The Condition of the Working Class in England*. It is ironical that this was written while Engels was enjoying board and lodging in his father's house. Since he was also helping Hess to organize public meetings to spread com-munist propaganda, friction was inevitable. Engels has left us a vivid description:

I am indeed living a dog's life here. All the religious fanati-cism of my old man has been aroused by the Communist meetings and by the 'dissolute character' of several of our local Communists with whom I am of course in close con-tact. And the old man's wrath has been increased by my firm refusal to go into petty trading. Finally my appearance in public as an avowed Communist has aroused in him a truly middle-class fury. Now try to put yourself in my place. Since I want to leave in a fortnight or so, I cannot afford to have a row. So I simply ignore all the criticisms of the family. They are not used to that so they get even angrier

. . . You can have no notion of the sheer malice that lies behind this wild Christian hunt after my 'soul'.

Tension got so bad that Engels eventually decided to join Marx in Brussels. The three subsequent years there were the only ones before his retirement when Engels could devote himself full time to political activities untroubled by the burden of his father's business.

They lived in adjoining houses and devoted themselves to the twin projects of working out in detail their newly-acquired views of the world, and getting them accepted by the nascent working-class movement. In the summer of 1846 the two friends made a trip to England, where Engels could act as Marx's guide, and on their return they jointly composed *The German Ideology* – a rich polemic against their former Young Hegelian colleagues, aiming at 'self-clarification' and containing probably the most extended description of their materalist conception of history that they ever wrote.

In order to get their views accepted, Engels and Marx had to make some impact on the German emigré workers' associations that flourished in Paris, Brussels and London, and replace the rather vague Utopian communism that had inspired them hitherto. According to a German worker of the time, Engels was 'tall and slim, his movements were quick and vigorous, his manner of speaking brief and decisive, his carriage erect, giving a soldierly touch. He was of a very lively nature; his wit was to the point. Everybody who associated with him inevitably got the impression that he was dealing with a man of great intelligence . . .' Still supported financially by his family, he spent several months proselytizing German workers in Paris, where the main emigré organization – the League of the Just – had originally operated. Its centre was now in

London and it was from there that an emissary arrived in early 1847 asking for the assistance of Engels and Marx in drafting a coherent theory and programme of action for the League. Engels went to London in June 1847 as Paris delegate to attend a Congress of the League and in November both he and Marx participated in a final session in which they were commissioned to draw up a Communist Manifesto – the League having meanwhile changed its name to the Communist League. Engels produced a first draft and Marx the final version, but before it could be distributed, the series of revolutions that shook most European countries during 1848 had begun in Paris.

After a brief stay in Paris, Engels and Marx settled in Cologne. The Communist League was dissolved as being unnecessary under the newly-granted freedom of association and speech, and the two friends turned their attention to journalism.

As Marx's main assistant on the *Neue Rheinische Zeitung*, Engels played an active role during 1848, the *annus mirabilis* of revolution in Europe. He was a radical journalist on a paper with wide and increasing circulation which aimed more at stiffening the opposition of the radical bourgeoisie to the monarchy than at directly promoting the working-class cause. His articles dealt mainly with foreign policy and his vividness of style and quick composition made him indispensable. By the autumn of 1848, however, the crisis of revolution in Germany had passed and Engels, who had been prominent in several anti-government demonstrations, fled to France as there was a warrant out for his arrest.

At a time when the counter-revolution was preparing decisive blows, Engels decided to embark on a walking tour of France. He made his leisurely way to Switzerland by way of the valleys of the Seine and Loire and the

Burgundy region. The ebullient description that he wrote of his travels combined insights into the profoundly conservative nature of the French peasantry with lyrical appreciations of his enjoyment of 'the sweetest grapes and loveliest of girls'.

Engels remained in Switzerland until mid-January 1849 when the possibility of arrest had diminished sufficiently for him to be able to return to Cologne. But the revolutionary wave was almost spent and the *Neue Rheinische Zeitung* was suppressed in May. There were desperate popular risings in the Rhineland and in Southern Germany and Engels returned to his hometown of Elberfeld to put his military expertise at the service of the insurgents. But the more middle-class elements of the citizen militia considered that Engels' presence might 'give rise to misunderstandings of the nature of the Movement' and he was asked to withdraw. (The story of Engels, red-sashed on an inspection of the artillery, meeting his father on his way to church is unconfirmed.) Engels made his way to the only remaining focus of armed resistance – the peasants and petty bourgeoisie of south-west Germany – and served as ADC to the rebel commander, Willich, throughout the forlorn campaign. After final defeat, Engels made his way to Genoa and took ship for London to join Marx in their exile.

Engels remained in London for one year. During that time he aided Marx's political activities on the Central Committee of the reconstituted Communist League. Although Chartism was almost dead and London was preparing for the Great Exhibition of 1851, Engels and Marx conserved for a brief period their optimism about the imminence of fresh revolutionary outbreaks on the Continent. However, by the autumn of 1850, Marx had come to the conclusion that such an event would have to wait on a fresh economic crisis, and therefore broke with those elements in the League which insisted on actively fomenting a revolution irrespective of the economic circumstances. Driven mainly by financial pressure, Engels decided to accede to his father's proposal that he join the family firm in Manchester. He arrived there in November 1850, aged 30. His expectation of a speedy return to London to participate in fresh revolutionary unheavals proved illusory: he was to stay in Manchester for the next two decades.

Engels' life in Manchester was essentially a double one, divided between business and communism. Manchester itself he hated and agreed with the Chartist leader Harney that it was better 'to be hanged in London than die naturally in Manchester'. The office work he found monotonous and time-consuming – although his position and status grew to be important. The firm of Ermen and Engels employed around 800 workers in the specialist process of manufacturing sewing thread. It was run by the brothers Peter and Godfrey Ermen, and Engels, although nominally only the senior clerk, aimed to make himself indispensable to his father by unofficially keeping an eye on the possible misuse of his father's capital. 'The difficulty was', he explained to Marx, 'to get an official position here as my father's representative over against the Ermens and yet have no official position inside the firm with consequent work obligations and salary from the firm.' What he termed his 'intrigue with my old man' was largely successful and by 1854 Engels had an annual salary plus a share in the profits that brought his annual income by the end of the 1850s to near £20,000 in present-day terms.

Engels lived for most of the time in a terraced house on the outskirts of the city with Mary Burns, an Irish working-class girl whom he had got to know on his first visit to

Manchester. Here he spent his spare evenings and week-ends as a revolutionary writer. However, he also maintained a bachelor lodgings in the centre of the city where he entertained his business friends. Engels knew how to divert himself, particularly through drinking: the teenage Eleanor Marx has a description of how, on a visit to Manchester during a heatwave, 'the ladies lay down on the floor the whole day, drinking beer, claret etc.' and that was how Engels found them on his return from work, 'all lying out full length on the floor, no stays, no boots, and one petticoat and a cotton dress on and that was all'. Engels returned from a party 'drunk as a jelly' and at least one of his friends 'got so sloshed that we had to make up a bed for him in the house'.

Engels' relationship with Mary Burns seems to have been a particularly happy one. When she died unexpectedly in 1864, he wrote to Marx: 'I cannot tell you what I feel. The poor girl loved me with all her heart . . . I feel that I have buried with her the last particle of my youth.' Soon afterwards, her younger sister Lizzie moved in to take her place. Lizzie, wrote Engels later, 'was of genuine Irish proletarian stock and her passionate innate feeling for her class was of far greater value to me and stood me in better stead at moments of crisis than all the refinement and culture of your educated and aesthetic young ladies'.

Engels also went in for several of the activities beloved of the Manchester bourgeoisie: he attended the Hallé concerts; he bought a fine stallion and rode regularly with the Cheshire Hunt; and he was a prominent member of two prosperous clubs – the Albert Club and the Schiller Institute, of which he eventually became Chairman. Several times a year Marx and Engels would stay with each other in London or Manchester; and Engels maintained a wide circle of friends in Manchester, including Dr Gumpert, a distinguished paediatrician, Samuel Moore, a barrister who was to translate *Capital* into English, and Karl Schorlemmer who held the first English Chair in Organic Chemistry.

This full social life was combined with considerable activity promoting the communist cause. Engels wrote regularly for the *New York Daily Tribune* under Marx's name as his friend had neither the time nor – initially – the necessary command of English. Engels wrote particularly on the Crimean War and on near- and far-eastern affairs, and also produced two major anti-Bonapartist pamphlets. This journalism was backed up by extremely wide reading in history and military science – including a considerable manuscript on Irish history that was never published. Engels also assiduously followed the latest developments in the natural sciences – for example, the discovery of the cell and the formulation of the laws of energy.

The pace of his life and business worries led to a breakdown in Engels' health – glandular fever, piles, and a nervous breakdown in 1860 which coincided with his father's death and the consequent negotiations over the future of the family business. His brother-in-law Emil Blank had to come over from Germany as Engels was, on his own account, 'incapable of taking a single necessary decision'. In the event, Jennie Marx's hope that Engels would become 'a great cotton-lord' was fulfilled: his father's legacy enabled him to put £10,000 of his own into the business and become a partner with a 20 per cent share of the profits and 5 per cent interest on his capital. Tension with the Ermen brothers nevertheless continued, and Engels was glad to be able to negotiate the end of his partnership in 1869. The terms enabled him to retire at the age of 50 and live the life of a gentleman of independent means. Eleanor Marx wrote:

> I was with Engels when he reached the end of his forced labour and I saw what he must have gone through all those years. I shall never forget the triumph with which he exclaimed 'for the last time!' as he put on his boots in the morning to go to his office. A few hours later we were standing at the gate waiting for him. We saw him coming over the little field opposite the house where we lived. He was swinging his stick in the air and singing, his face beaming. Then we set the table for a celebration and drank champagne and were happy.

On moving to London in 1870, Engels rented a sizeable house in Regents Park Road, about fifteen minutes' walk from Marx, whom he visited almost daily. Lizzie Burns died in 1878 – Engels married her on her deathbed – and her niece Pumps looked after his household. On Marx's death in 1883, his friends urged him to return to Germany. 'But,' he replied, 'my fifty years of service in the International Socialist Movement make it impossible for me to put myself forward as the representative of any one national socialist party', and he decided to remain in his 'peaceful asylum' in London. Helene Demuth acted as Engels' housekeeper for seven years to be replaced, finally, by Louise, ex-wife of Karl Kautsky, one of the young theoreticians of the German party. At weekends Engels entertained his London friends and kept open house for foreign visitors. Edward Aveling, Eleanor Marx's common-law husband, wrote that 'a list of those who were always welcome at 122 Regents Park reads like a condensed epitome of the Socialist Movement'.

At last freed from the burden of business, Engels could now devote himself full time to his twin pursuits of socialist scholarship and of being political adviser to the growing socialist parties. During the 1870s he spent 'the best part of eight years' studying science and mathematics, researches which led to the posthumously published manuscript on the *Dialectics of Nature*. His abiding interest in prehistory and anthropology led to a very popular work on *The Origin of the Family, Private Property and the State*, published in 1884. But his most widely disseminated book was the polemic of 1878 against the socialist intellectual Eugen Dühring which set out a systematic and comprehensive 'Marxist' interpretation of the world and, under the title *Anti-Dühring*, became the basic guide for a whole new generation of Marxists.

Engels' main efforts, however, went into editing Marx's drafts of *Capital*. On Marx's death, Engels was dismayed to learn how sketchy these drafts in fact were. He wrote to Bebel: 'If I had been aware of this, I would not have let him rest day or night until everything had been finished and printed. Marx himself knew this better than anyone.' Engels was the only person who could decipher Marx's illegible hieroglyphics; and, in spite of increasing trouble with his eyesight, he managed to complete Volume II, which he dictated to a secretary, by 1885. The more fragmentary Volume III proved much more difficult and eventually took ten years to complete. Before his death, Engels initiated Kautsky and Eduard Bernstein, the two leading Party intellectuals, into the mystery of Marx's handwriting, and it was Kautsky who later edited the *Theories of Surplus Value*, otherwise known as the fourth volume of *Capital*.

This scholarly research went hand in hand with close attention to the socialist movement. Engels' energies were particularly directed towards the German Socialist Party which, in spite of Bismarck's anti-socialist laws in the 1880s, had grown to one of the largest parties in Germany by the time of Engels' death. The German Social Democratic Party (SPD) had been founded in 1875 at the Gotha Congress and Engels, together with Marx, was vigorous in his criticisms of the concessions made in the programme to the followers of their great rival Ferdinand Lassalle. Engels had constantly, by letters and articles, to oppose the tendencies in the party to form a socialism based less exclusively on class struggle than he would have liked. In 1891, however, he had the satisfaction of helping to draw up for the Erfurt Congress a thoroughgoing Marxist programme. He also exercised a constant influence on the next generation of Marxist leaders: on Wilhelm Liebknecht, who had been Marx's and Engels' disciple from the 1840s; on August Bebel, a lathe operator from Saxony who became the main architect of the party's organization; on Eduard Bernstein, editor of the Party's newspaper and soon to be protagonist of the Revisionist movement; and on Karl Kautsky, a young journalist from Prague who was to be the Party's chief theoretician for the two decades after Engels' death. In addition, Engels maintained a worldwide correspondence. 'Every day, every post', wrote Marx's son-in-law Lafargue, 'brought to his house newspapers and letters in every European language, and it was astonishing how he found time, with all his other work, to look through, to keep in order and remember the chief contents of them all.'

Gradually, however, ill health undermined his capacity for work. Rheumatism, bronchitis and weak eyesight confined him to his bed sometimes for weeks on end. He was still capable of celebrating his 70th birthday in style: 'We kept it up till half-past-three in the morning and drank, besides Claret, sixteen bottles of champagne – in the morning we had twelve dozen oysters. So you see I did my best to show that I was still alive and kicking.' And Engels also travelled: in 1888 he visited the United States for two months and in 1892 his work for the Second International culminated in the triumphant reception accorded to him at the Zürich Congress. However, in the summer of 1895 it became clear that Engels had cancer of the throat and he died in August of the same year. He left most of his £30,000 to Marx's daughters. Eleanor inherited the letters and manuscripts of her father; the rest went to Bernstein and Bebel. In accordance with his wishes, Engels' body was cremated and his ashes scattered in the sea off Beachy Head.

2 History

It was in writing history that Engels' talents found their fullest expression. His gift for descriptive writing and his wide chronological and geographical interests, combined with his linguistic skills and flexibility in using his Marxist framework, made him into a first-rate historian. He produced an immense volume of articles on a wide range of topics, but his major contributions are three: his analysis of the English working class in the mid-1840s; his researches into prehistory; and his attempts to systematize the principles of historical materialism.

Engels' essay in contemporary history entitled *The Condition of the Working Class in England* arose directly out of his conversion to communism. In an article published in early 1844 (which had a decisive influence on Marx) Engels had already pungently summarized his critique of contemporary liberal economic theories. This article, entitled *Outlines of a Critique of Political Economy*, dealt with the fundamental categories of trade, value, rent and population, and claimed that economists attached to the idea of private property and competition could not give an adequate conceptual – still less an adequate moral – account of them: 'Economists cannot afford to accept the truth. They cannot afford to admit that the contradiction of wealth and poverty is simply the consequence of competition. Any such admission would result in the total collapse of their theories.' Engels' conclusion was that

under normal conditions, large capital and large landed

property swallow small capital and small landed property
. . . The middle classes must increasingly disappear until
the world is divided into millionaires and paupers, into
large landowners and poor farm labourers . . . Competition
has penetrated into all human relationships and it has
completed human bondage in all its aspects. Competition is
still the great mainspring which repeatedly jerks our dying
social order – or rather disorder – but with each newest
effort competition also saps a part of the waning strength of
our social system.

At the end of his article, Engels announced his intention
of describing the factory system. This he did in *The
Condition of the Working Class* which appeared early in
1845 and gave an extended account of the social impact of
industrialization at its most advanced point.

Engels' book began with a chapter on the Industrial
Revolution and its product – the industrial proletariat. It
was a powerful piece of writing, concise and coherent, only
marred, at the beginning, by a ridiculously idyllic picture
of the rural life of eighteenth-century England which
industrial progress had so largely replaced.

The third chapter on the great towns formed the centre-
piece of Engels' work. He started with London, and after
going through the major Yorkshire towns, concentrated
on the Manchester–Salford conurbation which contained
almost half a million people and formed the major industrial complex of England. Its wealth was centred on the
cotton trade in which about a third of its population was
directly employed. Engels produces his effect by a vivid
attention to detail of which the following extract is a
typical example. Describing that bit of Manchester known
as Little Ireland, Engels writes:

Masses of refuse, offal, and sickening filth lie among standing
pools in all directions; the atmosphere is poisoned by the

effluvia from these, and laden and darkened by the smoke of a dozen tall factory chimneys. A hoard of ragged women and children swarm about here, as filthy as the swine that thrive upon the garbage heaps and in the puddles. In short the whole rookery furnishes such a hateful and repulsive spectacle as can be hardly equalled in the worst court on the Irk. The race that lives in these ruinous cottages, behind broken windows, mended with oilskin, sprung doors, and rotten doorposts, or in dark, wet cellars, in measureless filth and stench, in this atmosphere penned in as if with a purpose, this race must really have reached the lowest stage of humanity.

And his general conclusion was that 'the working class of the great cities offers a graduated scale of conditions in life, in the best cases a temporarily endurable existence for hard work and good wages, good and endurable, that is, from the workers' standpoint; in the worst cases, bitter want reaching even homelessness and death by starvation. The average is much nearer the worst cases than the best.'

Engels then went on to describe the results accruing from these conditions. He detailed the diseases – particularly consumption – that produced 'pale, emaciated, narrow-chested and hollow-eyed ghosts'. (In Manchester over half the children of working-class parents died before the age of five.) He described the illiteracy that had its counterpart in bigotry and fanaticism, and the alcoholism that fostered sexual immorality and ever-increasing crime. There followed an account of the factory system with its exploitation of women and children as cheap labour, and its spate of accidents and spinal injuries. Engels particularly emphasized the power of the mill owners over their operatives, in everything from sexual favours to rent and the price of food in the factory-owned shops. He then dealt with the mines and the agricultural sector in the same manner. After a chapter on labour movements in which Engels took recent strikes as evidence that 'the decisive battle between the proletariat and the bourgeoisie is approaching', he discussed the attitude of the middle classes towards the workers, concentrating on their greed and hypocrisy as exemplified in the Poor Law. He concluded by declaring that only communism could overcome class antagonisms and heal the increasingly bitter social conflicts.

The Condition of the Working Class was a pioneering work in the relatively modern fields of urban geography and sociology, and Engels, although only 24 years old, was singularly well equipped to write it. Much of the impressiveness of the book springs from his evidently first-hand acquaintance with his material both as a business-man and through his active socialist contacts. Engels had a quite extraordinary gift for conveying in words his own personal experiences, and the descriptive passages of the book give it its main impact. He also made excellent use of government publications and statistics (much as Marx did in *Capital*). Although it has recently been argued on the basis of statistics that the working class was increasingly better off during the period Engels was describing, and that therefore his account is biased and unreliable, this view is extremely dubious and Engels' descriptions can be taken, by and large, as probably the best piece of contemporary evidence that we have available to us. Engels rightly claimed that his book was unique for its time in that it dealt with the English working class as a whole, but it went even further: his description of the working class was embedded in an analysis of the evolution of industrial capitalism which lent it a coherent historical, and to some extent conceptual, framework. For example, Engels was able here to deal at greater length with concepts that he had briefly mentioned in his *Outline* – the significance of the drive to larger and larger businesses, the reserve army of the unemployed that could be called on in times of expansion, and the periodicity of crises.

The main weakness of the book – which does not detract from its general value – was in its predictions. Engels talked, for example, of the speedy collapse of society being 'as certain as a mathematical or mechanical demonstration'. Such hasty statements were made under the impact of the worst slump of the nineteenth century – that of the early 1840s. In the event, of course, this crisis only proved to be the forerunner of a major boom in heavy industry – based mainly on railway expansion. In this respect, the best comment is that of Marx, some twenty years later:

> I have read your book again and I have realized that I am not getting any younger. What power, what incisiveness and what passion drove you to work in those days! That was a time when you were never worried by academic scholarly reservations! Those were the days when you made the reader feel that your theory would become hard fact, if not tomorrow then at any rate on the day after. Yet that very illusion gave the whole work a human warmth and a touch of humour that makes our later writings – where 'black and white' have become 'grey and grey' – seem positively distasteful.

Engels had an abiding interest in history of an exceptionally wide nature. For example, immediately following the failure of 1848, and in an attempt to understand its causes, he wrote an insightful series of articles on *The Peasant War in Germany*, arguing that there were startling resemblances between the combination of nobles and burghers in the sixteenth century to crush the peasants' revolt, and the eventual alliance in 1848 between the bourgeoisie and the aristocracy against the nascent proletariat. 'From 1517 to 1525', wrote Engels, 'Luther underwent quite the same changes as the present-day German constitutionalists did between 1846 and 1849, and which are undergone by every bourgeois party, which, placed for a while at the head of the movement, is overwhelmed by the plebeian proletarian party standing behind it.' His real hero was Thomas Münzer who 'went far beyond the immediate ideas and demands of the plebeian peasants and first organized a party of the elite of the then existing revolutionary elements which, inasmuch as it shared his ideas and energy, always remained only a small minority of the insurgent masses'.

His historical interests were also reflected in an impressive section of *Anti-Dühring*, devoted to refuting the Dühring view that force was the fundamental factor in historical development: the use of force was itself dependent on underlying economic conditions. Engels decided to republish this section in book form and added a very fine chapter on the role of force in the last three decades of German history. This dealt specifically with Bismarck's policy of uniting Germany on the basis of an alliance between the landowning aristocracy and the bourgeoisie and his final failure through relying excessively on the large landowners whose economic power was in decline.

Engels also became one of the very few civilian experts in the specialist field of military history and techniques. He had himself had military experience in the Baden rising of 1849 of which he wrote a brilliant descriptive account. During the 1850s Engels contributed numerous articles on military affairs to the press in America, Britain and Germany. In 1859 he enhanced his reputation in Germany by writing a pamphlet entitled *Po and Rhine* which argued that Germany's security could quite adequately be guaranteed without Austria's occupation of Northern Italy which merely served to alienate the Italians. In spite of his inaccurate prediction of the outcome both of the American Civil War and of the Franco–Prussian War of 1866, Engels made a great impression by the expertness of his articles on the Franco–Prussian War of 1870, published in the *Pall Mall Gazette*. He also drew up detailed plans for the Commune's defence of Paris. Lenin, in particular, was much influenced by Engels' writings on military affairs and on armed insurrection.

Engels' historical interests went farther back in time the older he got. Agrarian history – on which Marx considered him an expert – was a particular focus of his attention. These researches on primitive societies bore fruit in the *Origin of the Family, Private Property and the State*, published in 1884. It relied heavily on Lewis Morgan's book *Ancient Society*, published in 1877, on which Marx had been working for some considerable time before his death. Engels described his book as 'the execution of a bequest' in that he used Marx's notes – though Engels based himself much more exclusively on Morgan than did Marx, who viewed Morgan as one authority among others and concentrated more on the socio-political aspects of his work. According to Engels, 'Morgan in his own way had discovered afresh in America the materialist conception of history discovered by Marx forty years ago.' And he believed that Morgan's anthropological discoveries had 'the same importance for anthropology as Darwin's theory of evolution has for biology and Marx's theory of surplus value for political economy'. Basing himself on Morgan, Engels contrasted the communal nature of primitive society with the exploitative relationships that succeeded it. He enquired into the nature of the family and particularly the changing role of women and went on to account for the rise of the state as the instrument of an exploiting class.

E. – B

Engels

In brief, Engels' views on the development of the family are as follows. There were three principal forms of marriage which roughly corresponded to the three principal stages of human development: for the period of savagery, group marriage; for barbarism, pairing marriage; for civilization, monogamy supplemented by adultery and prostitution. Relying on Morgan's reconstruction of the primitive forms of family from systems of consanguinity, he postulated a situation in which unrestricted sexual freedom existed inside the tribe. This was then superseded by the consanguine family in which marriage groups were separated according to generation. This then gave rise to the punaluan family in which, following the prohibition of intercourse between brothers and sisters, there was common possession of husbands and wives within a family circle from which, however, the brothers of the wives (and sisters of the husbands) were excluded. It was this family structure that formed the basis of the *Gens* – a firm circle of blood relations in the female line among whom marriage was prohibited. Within the *Gens*, as the prohibition of marriage with blood relations grew ever more exclusive, group marriage gave rise to pairing marriage without, however, destroying the supremacy of women in the communistic household, or the high respect accorded to them as the only recognizable parents. For 'the communistic household, in which most or all of the women belonged to one and the same *Gens*, while the men came from various *Gentes*, is the material foundation of that supremacy of the women which was general in primitive times'.

With the advent of barbarism, characterized by the spread of agriculture and the domestication of animals, the position of the man became more important. Whereas previously, as the provider of food, he had simply owned his hunting weapons, now, in the same capacity, he owned cattle and (later) slaves. And since inheritance was in the female line, he found his own children disinherited. Thus the male line of descent and the paternal law of inheritance began to prevail. In a striking passage Engels wrote: 'The overthrow of mother right was the world historical defeat of the female sex.' With the establishment of the patriarchal family, the way was open for the establishment of monogamy which made the man supreme in the family and enabled him to propagate heirs to his wealth that were indisputably his own. Looking to the future, Engels declared:

full freedom of marriage can therefore only be generally established when the abolition of capitalist production and of the property relations created by it has removed all the accompanying economic considerations which still exert such a powerful influence on the choice of a marriage partner . . . What we can now conjecture about the way in which sexual relations will be ordered after the impending overthrow of capitalist production is mainly of a negative character, limited for the most part to what will disappear. But what will there be new? That will be answered when a new generation has grown up: a generation of men who never in their lives have known what it is to buy a woman's surrender with money or any other social instrument of power; a generation of women who have never known what it is to give themselves to a man from any other considerations than real love.

Moving from the family, Engels discussed a discovery of Morgan's that was 'at least as important as his reconstruction of the primitive family', i.e. that the *Gens* was an institution common to all barbarians until their entry into civilization and even afterwards. The *Gens* consisted of all persons who, in punaluan marriage, form the descendants of a particular ancestral mother. No member was permitted to marry within the *Gens* and since descent was in the female line only the offspring of daughters remained within the *Gens*, whereas offspring of the sons belonged to the *Gentes* of their mother. Its leaders were chosen and dismissible by all the members, and property remained within the *Gens*, whose members owed each other help and protection.

Engels was concerned to show that the *Gens* was also at the origin of Greek society and demonstrated how its destruction entailed the origin of the state – an institution which needed a territorial basis, a public force distinct from the people, and the power to raise taxes. Ancient Athens was a prime example of how 'the state developed, how the organs of the Gentile constitution were partly transformed in this development, partly pushed aside by the introduction of new organs, and last superseded entirely by real state authorities'. Progressive division of labour and the sale and purchase of land meant an increasing drive towards government based on territory rather than kinship.

> The growing money economy penetrated like a corrosive acid into the old traditional life of the rural communities founded on natural economy. The constitution based on the *Gens* is absolutely irreconcilable with money economy; the ruin of the Attic small farmers coincided with the loosening of the old bonds of the *Gens*, which embraced and protected them. The debtor's bond and the lien on property respected neither *Gens* nor phratry.

Engels traced the same process in ancient Rome and then among the Germans, ascribing their superiority over the later Roman empire to their Gentile constitution and the qualities that this encouraged.

Engels' book was strikingly original in turning the attention of socialists to the possibility that sexual and productive relations had in some respect been superior in primitive society. More specifically, the book constituted a substantial contribution to the study of the emancipation of women – considerably aided by Bebel's continuation of these themes in his popular *Women under Socialism*. It suffered, however, from its dependence on Morgan, whose Darwinist evolutionary perspective led him to posit a much too general scheme of evolution – particularly considering his almost total disregard for Asia and Africa. Given also that Morgan's ideas on primitive sexual promiscuity, group marriage, and the chronological priority of the matrilinear over the patrilinear *Gens* are extremely dubious, it is not surprising that the section on the family is the weakest part of Engels' book. More curious is his strict dichotomy between the production of the species on the one hand and the production of the means of existence on the other. This is exemplified in his view that monogamy was 'the first form of family to be based not on natural but on economic conditions' and in his contrast between natural selection in savage and barbaric society with new *social* forces that only emerged later – all of which seem to posit a most unMarxist division between the economic and the social.

Under the influence of his historical and anthropological studies, Engels was more willing than Marx to be specific about future communist society. His approach was characterized by his enthusiasm for the transforming power of industry and for evolutionary theories; there is less emphasis on the subjective elements of class struggle and consciousness. This tendency is evident in Engels' well-known statement that in future communist society 'the government of persons is replaced by the administration of things'; or again, in the view that communist society will be able to consign the whole state machinery 'into the museum of antiquities, next to the spinning wheel and the bronze axe'. But it is in his article *On Authority* that this view reaches its peak. Here he described the discipline necessary in communist society by using the model of a factory :

> the automatic machinery of a big factory is much more despotic than the small capitalists who employ workers ever have been. At least with regard to the hours of work one may write up on the portals of these factories : *Lasciate ogni autonomia, voi che entrate!** If man, by dint of his knowledge and inventive genius, has subdued the forces of nature, the latter avenge themselves upon him by subjecting him, insofar as he employs them, to a veritable despotism independent of all social organization. Wanting to abolish authority in large-scale industry is tantamount to wanting to abolish industry itself, to destroy the power loom in order to return to the spinning wheel . . . a revolution is certainly the most authoritarian thing there is.

> *Abandon all autonomy, ye who enter here!

Engels seemed to believe that the capitalist organization of industry was merely to be run by the workers in post-revolutionary society in a more effective way – rather than radically restructured through a process of social emancipation. Rationality, planning and the division of labour would remain and the productive process would still be geared quantitatively to maximum output as its overriding goal. Engels was also considerably influenced by Darwin and it is significant that his best-known pronouncement on the state in communist society – 'it is not abolished, it withers away' – embodied a metaphor drawn from biology. Even his famous statement that the socialization of the means of production would constitute 'humanity's leap from the realm of necessity into the realm of freedom' minimized the amount of necessity implicit in any real struggle for freedom.

Towards the end of his life, Engels found himself obliged to give an account of the basic principles of historical materialism – indeed the very phrase originates with him. With its growing popularity, the theory needed a clearer formulation than had hitherto been available. Marx and Engels had elaborated at length in *The German Ideology* the position that 'the nature of individuals depends on the material conditions determining their production'. But *The German Ideology* remained unpublished and Marx's *Preface* to a *Critique of Political Economy* of 1859 with its statement that 'the mode of production in material life determines the general character of the social, political and spiritual processes of life' was liable to misinterpretation. During the 1880s several young German historians had published pieces of research based on what they conceived to be the economic determinism of Marx. The crudity of their approach had laid them open to justified attack by non-Marxist historians. They then turned to Engels to ask for an authoritative statement on the determining factors in history. In his replies Engels' main point was to emphasize the mutual interaction of factors – always on the basis of the overriding importance of the economic. (The notion of the reciprocal interaction of various elements is prominent in his discussion of chemistry in the *Dialectics of Nature*, and Engels seems to have transferred it rather cavalierly from the natural sciences to the domain of history.) He was willing to admit that elements of the superstructure – ideologies, for example, or legal arrangements – did have a relative and circumscribed independence since they possessed structures and laws peculiar to themselves which could influence the basis and, indeed, in extreme instances, become temporarily the overall determining factor. Engels also admitted that 'Marx and I are ourselves partly to blame for the fact that the younger people sometimes lay more stress on the economic side than is due to it.' According to him, this was because 'we had to emphasize the main principle, vis-à-vis our adversaries, who denied it, and we had not always the time, the place, or the opportunity to allow the other elements involved in interaction to come into their right'. Summarizing his views, Engels declared:

> according to the materialist conception of history, the *ultimately* determining element in history is the production and reproduction of real life. More than this neither Marx nor I have ever asserted. Hence if somebody twists this into saying that the economic element is the only determining one, he transforms that proposition into a meaningless, abstract, senseless phrase. The economic situation is the basis, but the various elements of the superstructure – political forms of the class struggle and its results, to wit: constitutions established by the victorious class after a successful battle, etc., juridical forms, and then even the reflexes of all these actual struggles in the brains of the participants, political, juristic, philosophical theories, religious views and their further development in the systems of dogmas – also exercise their influence upon the course of the historical struggles and in many cases preponderate in determining their *form*. There is an interaction of all these elements in which, amid all the endless host of accidents (that is, things and events, whose inner connection is so remote or so impossible of proof that we can regard it as non-existent, as negligible) the economic movement finally asserts itself as necessary.

Some commentators have claimed that these statements of Engels constituted some sort of revision of the basic principles of Marxism. Indeed, Bernstein called on the authority of Engels to buttress his overtly revisionist views. No doubt Engels' pronouncements did run contrary to certain vulgarizations of Marxism, but not to Marx himself, who was not much given to general theoretical pronouncements on historical materialism – except, perhaps, in his famous 1859 *Preface* to the *Critique of Political Economy*. It is, nevertheless, true to say that Engels' statements did represent a somewhat different and more jejune approach by attempting to isolate the 'economic factor' and oppose it to other factors in a way that robbed it of the social and historical content that it tended to have in Marx.

3 Politics

Engels' early political views changed considerably as he progressed from his Pietist background through Young Hegelian idealism to communism. Brought up in the industrial towns of the Ruhr, he was well acquainted with the social problems caused by early industrialization. But his close contact with the Young Hegelians and the fact that he was converted to communism by Moses Hess meant that his revolutionary ideas still contained a large mixture of idealism and Feuerbachian humanism. His move to England meant a move from the philosophical speculation of Germany to a closer study of the reality of social and political conditions. Engels was impressed by Chartism and by the Owenites. He wrote an appreciative essay on Carlyle's *Past and Present* and *Outlines of a Critique of Political Economy*, which Marx much later still recognized as a 'sketch of genius'.

Towards the end of 1843 Engels formulated his notion of communism as follows:

Thus the three large civilized countries of Europe – England, France and Germany – have all come to the conclusion that a thoroughgoing revolution of social relationships on the basis of a community of property has now become an urgent and unavoidable necessity. This result is all the more impressive as each of the three above-mentioned nations has come to it independently from the others; there can be no stronger proof available than this that Communism is not merely the consequence of a particular situation of the English or any other nation but a necessary consequence which must inevitably be drawn from presuppositions that are given in the general conditions of modern civilization.

It is striking that Engels, even after his close contact with the Manchester working class as evidenced in his *Condition of the Working Class*, could still say that 'Communism stands, in principle, above the reach between the bourgeoisie and the proletariat . . . Communism is a question of humanity and not of the workers alone.' Thus for Engels, even as late as 1845, revolution meant the victory of principles in some way immanent in the historical process over the irrational and chaotic present. If society were not rationally ordered, then the ever-increasing contradictions in it would bring about disasters and catastrophes that would force a total upheaval. Communism was in some way above class and could appeal on rational grounds to all individuals with the capacity for insight into the social process. The vocation of the communist thinker was to make these rational grounds plain to all in the hope of forwarding the cause of communism and avoiding a social catastrophe.

It was his collaboration with Marx in 1845 – particularly in *German Ideology* – that enabled Engels to give these rather idealistic political principles a much sharper focus in socio-economic reality. The years 1846–9 were politically the most active years of Engels' life. After clarifying their ideas in *The German Ideology*, Marx and Engels set to work to implant these ideas in the German artisan movement. Engels agitated among the German workers in Paris and Brussels; he acted as chief negotiator with the leaders of the Communist League in London; he was the right-hand man of Marx on the staff of *Neue Rheinische Zeitung*; and he finished up the revolutionary year as an active participant in the Baden campaign. Theoretically, Engels made two main contributions at this time: the first was the formulation of a basic communist outlook, chiefly in the *Principles of Communism* which formed the basis for the famous *Communist Manifesto*: and the second was his articles for the *Neue Rheinische Zeitung*.

The *Principles of Communism* was a summary of Engels' work over the previous years in the *Condition of the Working Class*, in his numerous political articles, and in *The German Ideology. The Principles of Communism* was clear, expository, and didactic, cast in the form of a catechism of twenty-five questions. Communism was 'the doctrine of the conditions for the emancipation of the proletariat'. The proletariat was that group which (unlike previous slaves, serfs, or artisans) got its livelihood solely by means of selling its labour. The industrial revolution had so mechanized production that basically only two classes remained in society: the capitalists and the proletariat, who received no more than a subsistence wage. Unbridled competition had led to crises in the economy, anarchical production, the growth of the proletariat, and the depression of wages – a state of affairs only to be overcome by the imposition of a fixed plan by the whole of the society in the interests of all. This would involve the abolition of private ownership – the lynchpin of communism. Such a revolution would have to be international, probably violent, and involve the introduction of a democratic constitution. Engels sketched out the kind of programme a victorious proletariat would introduce, and went on to give an outline of communist society. A vast increase in productivity would mean sufficient goods for all and the possibility of the abolition of the division of labour. There would be no antagonism between town and country. Communism would also involve the abolition of the dependency of wives on husbands and children on parents, the overcoming of national boundaries, and the rendering obsolete of religion. He finished with a summary of the differences between communists and other socialists and an account of the attitude of communists to contemporary political parties.

The emphasis in Engels' document lay on the historically necessary consequences of the industrial revolution. It was inferior in style to *The Communist Manifesto*, and lacked the preoccupation with political consciousness and class structure that a closer acquaintance with French socialism and Hegelian dialectics had given to Marx. Above all, it lacked the impressive power of synthesis in overall design that made *The Communist Manifesto* so striking. Nevertheless, the *Principles of Communism* remains important as the first fundamental statement of communist policy.

At the end of *Principles of Communism* Engels had said that, as far as Germany was concerned, 'it is in the interests of the Communists to help bring the bourgeoisie to power as soon as possible in order to overthrow them again'. In order to achieve this aim, Marx and Engels put their main effort during the revolutionary years of 1848–9 into the creation and running of a newspaper that would support a 'united front' of all democratic forces. Its programme was universal suffrage, direct elections, the abolition of all feudal dues and charges, the establishment of a state banking system, and the admission of state responsibility for employment.

The cause of the emancipation of the bourgeoisie meant that the paper did not, at least initially, deal with the situation or interests of the working class as such. Engels dealt principally with foreign policy, the main point of which was a revolutionary war against Russia on the model of the French Revolutionary offensive against feudal Germany after 1789. Such a war, he considered, would crush the most conservative regime in Europe, restore Polish independence, and internally lead to the creation of a unitary state in Germany.

On his return to Cologne in early 1849 after three months' exile Engels saw his hopes of revolution in England dashed, but was still optimistic about Hungary and France. He turned his attention particularly to the course of the revolution in the Austro–Hungarian empire and came to the unMarxist view that victory of the Germans and Hungarians over 'minor' or 'history-less' Slav nations was equivalent to the victory of civilization over barbarism. Support for the German bourgeoisie meant support for the Polish and Hungarian nobility that were aligned with them, and this led Engels to write – with a strain of German chauvinism that never quite deserted him :

> Among all the nations of Austria there are only three that have had any active impact on history and which are still capable of life – the Germans, the Poles and the Magyars. Therefore they are now revolutionary. All other large and small races and people have the immediate mission of going under in the world-revolutionary storm. Therefore they are at present counter-revolutionary.

That this view of Engels' was not an isolated one is shown by his approval of the recent American annexation of Californian goldmines belonging to Mexico. This piece of imperialism was justified by Engels on the grounds that the 'energetic Yankees' were more capable than 'lazy Mexicans' of developing the productive potential of the Pacific Ocean seaboard.

Only at the very end of the revolutionary movement, in April 1849, did Marx and Engels abandon their support for the bourgeoisie and advocate the creation of a separate workers' party. For eighteen months after the failure of the revolution they continued to be active in the Communist League and maintained their optimism over the imminence of a revolutionary revival. It then became clear to them, however, that this would have to wait on a fresh economic crisis. In a series of articles written in 1851, entitled *Revolution and Counter-Revolution in Germany*, Engels summed up the lessons learned from the recent German Revolution. He gave a very clear view of the underdeveloped nature of the German economy, of the importance of land tenure, and of the historical reasons for the lack of a really solid bourgeois class.

The 1850s and 1860s were the years of lowest ebb in Engels' political activities. He had withdrawn from the febrile squabbles of refugee politics in England. Conservative reaction had established itself firmly on the continent of Europe with little or no organized opposition. Engels therefore confined himself to the writing of articles most of which had only an indirectly political nature. This situation began to change in the mid-1860s with the formation of the First International, a loose confederation of parties, trade unions and individuals designed to promote working-class interests on an international scale. However, he was only active in the International during the two years prior to its disintegration in 1872. During 1864 to 1870 Marx in London had little help from Engels in Manchester who was, in any case, sceptical about the efficacy of the International at its outset. Engels joined as a member but did not organize any branch. In 1870, on his moving to London, Engels was elected to a seat on the General Council and devoted most of his time to its activities during the ensuing two years. He was chosen to be corresponding secretary for Spain and Italy and was active in opposing the spread of Bakunin's ideas. However, Engels got on much less well with the English Trade Unionists (who disliked his 'Prussian' attitude) than did Marx, and this hampered his effectiveness.

During the last twenty years of his life Engels came into his own as a political leader. By the late 1870s the various European socialist parties were recovering strongly from the setbacks of the Commune and the dissolution of the International. Engels was their natural mentor and point of liaison – 'the leader of the orchestra' as he called himself, fulfilling the role of the international socialist bureau which was only created after his death. By temperament and provenance, the socialist party to which Engels felt himself closest was the German Social Democratic Party over which he exercised a continuous, and at times almost chauvinistic, guardianship. Liebknecht, Bebel, Bernstein, Kautsky – all had sat at his feet and with all he kept up a constant correspondence. The party had been formed by a fusion of the followers of Lassalle with those of Marx's disciples Liebknecht and Bebel at the Gotha Congress of 1875. Engels and Marx considered that far too many concessions had been granted to the Lassalleans, but became more reconciled to the Party leadership as Marxist theory became increasingly influential in its ranks. This process culminated in the Erfurt Congress of 1891. Just prior to the Congress, Engels published Marx's criticisms of Lassalle in his *Critique of the Gotha Programme* in order to 'settle accounts between Marx and Lassalle'. He commented extensively on the draft for the Programme drawn up by Liebknecht, Kautsky and Bernstein, and saw his ideas largely accepted.

Between Engels and the SPD leadership there was the inevitable tension of theoretician in exile and practical politicians in the field. But they shared an optimism concerning the inevitable growth and imminent victory of their Party. During the 1870s, Engels accepted a basic division of labour between Marx and himself; Marx was to devote himself to finishing his *magnum opus* while Engels was to champion and defend in print their views against all opponents. In this he was eminently successful: *Anti-Dühring* was very popular and the three chapters reprinted from it under the title *Socialism, Utopian and Scientific* were translated into more languages than any other socialist work – including *The Communist Manifesto*.

Engels was particularly vigilant in opposing the intrusion of tendencies which 'wished to expunge the class struggle from the movement' and 'openly state that the workers are too uneducated to emancipate themselves and must be freed from above by philanthropic big bourgeois and petty bourgeois'. Although Bismarck's anti-socialist legislation forced the Party into semi-clandestinity throughout the 1880s, Engels produced a constant stream of articles for the banned publications of the SPD. In the event, this period of persecution radicalized the Party and assisted the establishment of Marxism (as interpreted by Engels) as its official policy. It also strengthened its following: votes increased steadily from 493,000 with twelve seats in the Reichstag in 1877 to almost 2 million votes and forty-four seats by 1893. Encouraged by this progress, Engels predicted in 1891 that the Party would come to power in 1898. This victory was mathematically calculable and he even had a graph to prove it. He was particularly impressed by the growth of socialist thought in the army. 'Even today', he wrote in 1892, 'one soldier in five is a socialist and within a few years there will be one in three. By the end of the century the ranks of the army – once the stronghold of Prussianism in Germany – will be filled with socialists. Nothing can withstand the fateful march of events.'

This belief in the march of events and the widespread

view in the Party that Marxism had shown the inevitability of the growth and victory of proletarian power led to an emphasis on peaceful rather than revolutionary attitudes which Engels did a lot to foster. The notion of revolution merged with that of the collapse of capitalism – a world that was not to be overthrown but inherited. But although for the Party leaders the renunciation of violence tended to become absolute and thus led them to put all their trust either in gaining a parliamentary majority (Bernstein) or in the automatic collapse of capitalism (Bebel), for Engels this abstinence remained much more of a tactic. The difference is well illustrated by the introduction that Engels wrote in 1895 to a re-edition of Marx's pamphlet *The Class Struggles in France*. As Engels died a few months after the publication, the article was viewed by many as his political testament. Bernstein, in particular, laid great emphasis on it as supporting his own revisionist doctrine of 'peaceful transition to socialism'. Engels had indeed declared in his article that 'the mode of struggle of 1848 is obsolete in every respect'. Commenting on the views that he and Marx had held in the 1840s, Engels admitted that 'history has not merely dispelled the erroneous notions we then held; it has also completely transformed the conditions under which the proletariat has to fight'. The franchise had been 'transformed from a means of deception, which it was before, into an instrument of emancipation'. The corollary of this was that

in Latin countries, also, it is being realized more and more that the old tactics must be revised. Everywhere the German example of utilizing the suffrage, of winning all posts accessible to us, has been imitated; everywhere the unprepared launching of an attack has been relegated to the background . . . Slow propaganda work and parliamentary activity are recognized . . . as the immediate tasks of the Party.

Engels laid great stress on the increasing mass membership of the SPD and on the 'firm muscles and rosy cheeks' that it was gaining under legal conditions: 'To keep this growth going without interruption until it of itself gets beyond the control of the prevailing governmental system, not to fritter away this daily increasing shock force in vanguard skirmishes but to keep it intact until the decisive day, that is our main task.' Bernstein – and the majority of his fellow-Marxists agreed with him – declared that Engels 'more clearly than ever before extolled universal suffrage and parliamentary activity as the means of working-class emancipation and rejected the idea of the conquest of political power through revolutionary upheaval'.

Only recently has it become clear that the more 'revolutionary' passages in Engels' article were cut out by the cautious Berlin leadership and that he only allowed it to be published in this form under protest. 'I am of the opinion', he wrote, 'that you gain nothing by preaching a complete abstinence from violence. No one believes it and *no* party in any country goes as far as to give up the right to withstand illegality arms in hand.'

Nevertheless, although Engels did not revise his opinion of the relationship between legality and revolution as radically as some have claimed, his attitude to SPD politics was seriously misconceived on several counts. Firstly, although having the revolutionary aims of the Party more clearly in mind than his colleagues inside Germany, he did posit an almost unbridgeable gap between present policies and revolutionary ends – a gap exemplified by the dichotomy into these two separate halves (theoretical and practical) of the Erfurt Programme of 1891 of which he was one of the direct architects. Secondly, Engels had too schematic a view of the bourgeoisie. For him, the immediate task of the SPD was so to organize itself that it could put pressure on the bourgeoisie to remain true to their own liberal principles. For the political freedom thus acquired could only help the development of the proletariat. But he overestimated the bourgeoisie's eagerness for reform and took little account of its readiness for compromise with the ruling powers. Nor was Engels in close touch with attitudes of the rank and file of his own party of which a high proportion of members were petty-bourgeois – at least in their outlook. He did not see that the Party organization, the trade union establishment, and indeed many ordinary Party members would have too much to lose in any future revolutionary upheaval. The number of industrial workers – i.e. proletarians in the strict sense – was a small minority. The fact that Engels' knowledge of the SPD was limited to its leaders led him to neglect the importance of economic struggle: his scorn for British trade unions and dismissal of the idea of a general strike led him to pose a stark alternative of legal activities or barricades and have little interest in decentralized, grassroots activities.

But Engels by no means confined his attention to Germany, and his correspondence with leading European socialists demonstrates how generally flexible and well informed he was as a political strategist. He was a close friend of Viktor Adler and gave him continual support and advice in his guiding and founding the Austrian Social Democratic Workers' Party. In France, he gave continuous assistance, including financial, to Guesde and Lafargue in their effort to create a viable Marxist Party – though here his efforts were less successful, as the socialist movement was divided into several factions. In Italy Engels maintained a close correspondence with Labriola, Italy's most distinguished Marxist thinker, and with Turati, founder of the Italian Workers' Party.

But it was Britain, naturally, that claimed, after Germany, Engels' main attention. During the 1850s and 1860s, his work at Ermen and Engels prevented him from taking part in political demonstrations or giving active support to the declining Chartist movement. He was, in any case, disgusted at the tendency of Chartist leaders to support alliances with the Liberals and concluded that

> the English proletariat is becoming more and more bourgeois, so that this most bourgeois of all nations is apparently aiming ultimately at the possession of a bourgeois aristocracy and a bourgeois proletariat as well as a bourgeoisie. For a nation which exploits the whole world this is, of course, to a certain extent, justified.

With the advent of the International, Engels switched his attention more to the trade unions, but in 1879 he was forced to state that 'there is no point in denying that, at the moment, no genuine Labour movement in the Continental sense exists in England'. There was a re-emergence of working-class unrest in the mid-1880s, but Engels remained critical both of Hyndman's Social Democratic Federation with its curious mixture of historical materialism, class struggle and jingoistic imperialism, and of the Socialist League of Belfort Bax and William Morris. 'The workers', he wrote, 'gaily share the feast of England's monopoly of the world market and colonies . . . a really general workers' movement will come into existence here only when the workers feel that England's world monopoly is broken.'

Engels' influence among English socialists was partly diminished by his support for Edward Aveling, Eleanor

Marx's common-law husband, who had, according to George Bernard Shaw, 'absolutely no conscience about money or women'. Eleanor and Aveling, however, achieved a considerable amount in organizing unions of unskilled labourers in the East End and supporting such manifestations of working-class unrest as the Dock Strike of 1889. This activity caught Engels' imagination and he declared that 'the revival of the East End of London remains one of the greatest and most fruitful facts of this *fin de siècle* and proud I am to have lived to see it'. However, the emergence of a strong workers' party in England was delayed until after his death – and then it developed along lines alien to his thought.

After the end of the International, Engels began, for the first time, to be seriously interested in the possibilities of revolution in Russia. He had always had an antipathy to the Slavs in general and Russia had been, for him, nothing more than the bulwark of European reaction. Nor had his hopes of Russia been improved by contact with such as Bakunin. By the mid-1870s, however, his mastery of the language and contact with Russian emigrés in London encouraged him to express an optimistic opinion of Russia's future in his controversy with the Populist leader Peter Tkachev. In common with most other Populists, Tkachev believed that a sufficiently determined minority could, by terrorist conspiracy, overthrow the Czarist regime and introduce a socialism based on the omnipresent peasant commune, thereby bypassing any capitalist stage of development. Engels was more inclined to believe in the necessity of a thoroughgoing bourgeois revolution in Russia as the next stage, and denied any independent vitality to the peasant commune. 'It is clear', he wrote, that communal ownership in Russia is long past its flourishing period and to all appearances is moving towards its dissolution. Nevertheless, the possibility undeniably exists of transforming this social form into a higher one . . . This, however, can happen only if, before the complete break-up of communal ownership, a proletarian revolution is successfully carried out in Western Europe.

It is ironical that, just at the moment when certain Populists – the young Plekhanov, for example – were moving towards Marxism, Engels became more sympathetic to Populism. Marx himself compared the Russian Marxist emigrés in Geneva unfavourably with the Populist activists inside Russia and, in an ambivalent reply to Plekhanov's colleague Vera Sassoulitch, had encouraged the Populists' hopes – a view reiterated in the 1882 Preface to the Russian *Communist Manifesto*. A few years later, Engels wrote to the same lady in a similar vein, giving a cool reception to Plekhanov's anti-Populist work *Our Differences*. The Russians, he declared, were approaching their 1789. 'The revolution *must* break out there in a limited period of time; it *may* break out any day. In these circumstances the country is like a charged mine which only needs a match to be applied to it. This is one of the exceptional cases where it is possible for a handful of people to *make* a revolution.' Engels overestimated the strength of the Populists and considered that the criticisms of Plekhanov and his friends only served to weaken the revolutionary opposition. By 1894, however, he once again came down strongly on the side of the Marxists, by admitting the demise of the commune as a viable institution and thus denying any possibility of uniqueness to Russia's future development. And this view formed the basis of Lenin's major work *The Development of Capitalism in Russia* written two years later.

4 Philosophy

Engels' most distinctive contribution to Marxism was his systematization of a would-be scientific Marxist 'philosophy'. This he did in three main works. The first – and most immediately influential – was *Anti-Dühring* (1877–8), in which Engels sought to refute the views of Eugen Dühring, a Berlin socialist who had recently attacked Marx's ideas as not being straightforwardly materialist, and who was becoming increasingly influential among many of Marx's German disciples. The second was an essay entitled *Ludwig Feuerbach and the Outcome of Classical German Philosophy* (1888), which Engels described as 'a short coherent account of our relation to the Hegelian philosophy, of how we proceeded, as well as of how we separated, from it'. The third was a work only published after Engels' death, though written mainly in the mid-1870s, entitled *Dialectics of Nature*, in which Engels attempted to work out a fundamental Marxist philosophy based on the idea that nature itself moved dialectically.

There were two general factors that influenced Engels' development of a general world outlook strongly orientated towards science. The more widespread the socialist movement became, the more need there was of a clear philosophical statement to guide the Party members – particularly as there were already rival systems in the field. And, quite naturally, the systematic orientation provided by Engels was strongly influenced by the growing preoccupation with scientific methodology in England and Germany and the growing prestige of natural science among large sections of society – not least the members of the SPD. Engels devoted a considerable portion of his time during the last two decades of his life to the study of natural science. After retiring from business in 1870, he wrote, 'I went through as complete as possible a "moulting", as Herr Liebig calls it, in mathematics and the natural sciences, and spent the best part of eight years on it.' What struck Engels as of particular importance were the discovery of the transformation of energy, the discovery of the cell as the basic unit of biological change, and the evolutionary theory of Darwin. These interests inevitably influenced Engels' presentation of his 'world view' and made him emphasize a dialectical conception of nature rather than of history. In particular, the work of Darwin made a profound impression on him and, as a result, he came in for considerable criticism from fellow Marxists for applying to society concepts drawn from biology. A corollary was that some of Engels' writings were directed just as much at scientists as at educated members of the working class; indeed he believed that 'the more ruthlessly and disinterestedly science proceeds the more it finds itself in harmony with the interests and aspirations of the workers'.

Engels was also led, paradoxically, to adopt some of the positions of his opponents, particularly in his *Anti-Dühring*. (The *Dialectics of Nature* was also originally conceived of as an 'Anti-Büchner' – Ludwig Büchner being at the time a very influential propagandist of the vulgar materialism that wished to reduce everything to the movement of matter.) In spite of his contempt for Dühring's 'system creating' Engels nevertheless said in his Preface that 'the polemic was transformed into a more or less connected exposition of the dialectical method and of the Communist world outlook'. Given the increasing popularity in socialist circles

Engels

of the naïvely materialist evolutionary concepts pro-
pounded by such thinkers as Dühring, Büchner, Vogt and
Haeckel, Engels was tempted to outbid them 'in order to
prevent a new occasion for sectarian divisions and con-
fusion from developing within the Party', and thus ended
up by merely offering a 'superior' form of materialist
monism.

The two most striking themes of _Anti-Dühring_ were
materialism and dialectics, and particularly the emphasis
on matter – a concept hitherto unemployed by Marx and
Engels. In _Anti-Dühring_ Engels talked of 'the materiality
of all existence' and said that 'both matter and its mode
of existence, motion, are uncreatable and . . . therefore
their own final cause'. At the same time, however, Engels
claimed that his materialism differed from the 'simple
metaphysical and exclusively mechanical materialism of
the eighteenth century . . . in opposition to this conception modern materialism embraces the more recent
advances in natural science . . .' It is the first of the three
sections of _Anti-Dühring_ that is of philosophical interest
(the other two deal with economics and socialism). Here
Engels set himself to apply 'conscious dialectics' to the
'materialist conception of nature and history'. He was
convinced that 'in nature, amid the welter of innumerable
changes, the same dialectical laws of motion force their
way through as those which in history govern the apparent
fortuitousness of events'. Engels began by contrasting metaphysical views – which looked on objects and ideas as
static and separate – with dialectics which emphasized
change and connection. Hegel, as the great protagonist of
dialectical thought, had the great merit of presenting 'for
the first time the whole world, natural, historical, intellectual, as a process, i.e. as in constant motion, change,
transformation, development'. But Hegel was an idealist,

and modern materialism, by contrast, said Engels, although essentially dialectical,

> no longer needs any philosophy standing above the other sciences. As soon as each special science is impelled to make clear its position in the great totality of things and of our knowledge of things, a special science dealing with this totality is superfluous. That which still survives, independently, of all earlier philosophy is the science of thought and its laws – formal logic and dialectics. Everything else is subsumed in the positive science of nature and history.

Engels then continued, by means of criticizing Dühring, to develop his own ideas. Man was a product of nature and man's consciousness, as a product of his brain, was also a product of nature which was merely reflected in men's minds. Knowledge was essentially limited, for 'each mental image of the world's system is and remains in actual fact limited, objectively by the historical conditions and subjectively by the physical and mental constitution of its originator'. Basing himself on the example of mathematics, Engels showed that all knowledge was empirical and had to begin with the actual world. In subsequent chapters he declared that the unity of the world consisted in its materiality, and attempted to show that space and time were infinite. He supported the Kantian notion of the origin of celestial bodies from rotating nebular masses, and investigated the concepts of motion and matter as basic to the understanding of physics and chemistry. The origin of life was to be accounted for on Darwinian principles.

Engels then proceeded to deny the existence of any 'eternal truths' either in science, history or ethics. The problem of freedom he viewed essentially along Hegelian lines of necessity's only being blind as long as it was not understood: freedom was the recognition of necessity.

Engels was, however, sufficiently tentative to admit that:

> how young the whole of human history still is, and how
> ridiculous it would be to attempt to ascribe any absolute
> validity to our present views, is evident from the simple fact
> that all past history can be characterized as the history of
> the epoch from the practical discovery of the transformation
> of mechanical motion into heat up to that of the transforma-
> tion of heat into mechanical motion.

He finished the section with a brief description of the laws
of the dialectic.

In the *Dialectics of Nature*, the links of natural science
with dialectics are much expanded. The surviving manuscripts begin with a look at the development of modern
science and then meditate on the origins of the solar
system and foresee a time when

> the declining warmth of the sun will no longer suffice to
> melt the ice thrusting itself forward from the poles; when
> the human race crowding more and more about the equator
> will finally no longer find even there enough heat for life;
> when gradually even the last trace of organic life will
> vanish; and the earth, an extinct frozen globe like the moon,
> will circle in deepest darkness and in an ever narrower orbit
> about the equally extinct sun, and at last fall into it. Other
> planets will have preceded it, others will follow it; instead
> of the bright warmth of the solar system with its harmonious
> arrangement of members, only a cold, dead sphere will still
> pursue its lonely path through universal space.

This rather bleak prospect is counter-balanced by 'the
certainty that matter remains eternally the same in all its
transformations, that none of its attributes can ever be lost,
and therefore, also, that with the same iron necessity that
it will exterminate on the earth its highest creation, the
thinking mind, it must somewhere else and at another time

again produce it'.

After a brief excursus on Victorian spiritualists, Engels described the familiar laws of the dialectic. He then devoted a chapter to the concept of motion and its basic forms. Motion was 'the mode of existence, the inherent attribute, of matter, and comprehends all changes and processes occurring in the universe, from mere change of place right up to thinking'. According to Engels, a truly dialectical view demonstrated the twin propositions that matter was indestructible and uncreated, and that motion had no beginning and no end. In the main body of the work, these ideas were worked out by investigating the latest researches in energy, tidal friction, heat and electricity. Basic to all these forms of motion was reciprocal interaction : thus natural science 'confirms what Hegel has said, that reciprocal action is the true *causa finalis* of things. We cannot go back further than to knowledge of this reciprocal action for the very reason that there is nothing behind it to know. If we know the forms of motion of matter, then we know matter itself, and therewith our knowledge is complete.' Engels here flirted with a view of matter that had affinities with German romantic philosophy such as that of Schelling and with contemporary life-force theories. This involved investing matter with what looked like a covert spiritualization. For although Engels talked about his views being 'not a philosophy at all any more, but simply a *Weltanschauung* which has to establish itself and prove itself in the real sciences', yet he introduced a profoundly teleological element into his thinking by claiming that it lay in the essence of matter to evolve into thinking beings.

Integral to Engels' material conception of nature was his epistemology. For Engels, man's knowledge of the external world consisted of 'reflections' or 'more or less abstract pictures of actual things and processes' and concepts were 'merely the conscious reflex of the dialectical motion of the real world'. Or again: 'Dialectics, so-called objective dialectics, prevails throughout nature, and so-called objective dialectics, dialectical thought, is only the reflection of the motion through opposites which asserts itself everywhere in nature.' At the same time, Engels was far from wishing to abandon entirely the doctrine of the unity of theory and practice: indeed, somewhat paradoxically, the pithiest formulation of this doctrine – Marx's *Theses on Feuerbach* – was first published by Engels as an appendix to his own *Ludwig Feuerbach*. Engels' idea of what was involved in the unity of theory and practice, however, was sometimes rather anaemic, as when he summarized it as 'experimentation and industry'.

Central also to Engels' materialism was his understanding of Hegel. For the later Engels, Hegel was a thinker 'of the greatest genius' who stood 'in the same relation to consciously dialectical natural science as the Utopians to modern Communism'. There is indeed a certain similarity between the system-building of the older Hegel and Engels' tendency to systematize Marxism on a natural scientific basis. But it could plausibly be claimed that Hegel had more of a genuine subject-object dialectic than Engels: Hegel, too, believed that there was a dialectic in nature – but that it was subject to the universal mediation of spirit. He thus conserved the subjective side of the dialectic so lacking in Engels. For Engels, like Marx, 'inverted' Hegel by putting his idealist philosophy on a materialist basis, but the result was not the idea that philosophy could be abolished by being put into practice that was so characteristic of their thinking in the 1840s. Engels entertained no notion that philosophy might possess a content to be realized; for he anticipated a time when philosophy in this sense would be entirely superseded. What Engels aimed at was the construction of a systematic materialism as all-embracing as Hegel's own system; and it is scarcely an over-simplification to say that this centrally involved the replacement of 'spirit' by 'matter' as the Absolute.

The exact relationship of the dialectic to this 'matter' was not clear. Engels claimed that the dialectical view of the world was indicated by the existence in things of 'contradictions'. For example, the notion of the square root of minus one was contradictory in itself, in that it was contradictory that a negative quantity should be the square of anything. More specifically, Engels defended Marx for his use of the law of the transformation of quantity into quality by pointing to the example of water which, at a certain temperature, turned into steam. Or again, Marx's use of the negation of the negation was illustrated by Engels through the example of the grain of barley which must perish in order to give rise to the plant. However, Engels explained,

> by characterizing the process as the negation of the negation, Marx does not intend to prove that the process was historically necessary. On the contrary: only after he has proved from history that in fact the process has partially already occurred and partially must occur in the future, he in addition characterizes it as a process which developed in accordance with a definite dialectical law.

Engels foresaw a time when the search for 'absolute truth' would be abandoned and instead 'the attainable relative truths will be pursued through the positive sciences and the summarizing of their results by means of dialectical thought'. But this is somewhat to downgrade the importance of the dialectic, suggesting that it is simply a re-description of facts and theories available without its help.

Engels believed that the principal 'laws' of the dialectic could be clearly formulated – and that this had first been achieved by Hegel. These, Engels said in *Dialectics of Nature*, 'can be reduced in the main to three: the law of the transformation of quantity to quality and vice versa; the law of the interpenetration of opposites; the law of the negation of the negation'. It is obviously only in the vaguest sense that these could be called 'laws'. (It may be significant that they are not given the typical formulation of laws, i.e. 'all quantities when sufficiently increased undergo a qualitative change'.) There is difficulty, for example, in identifying, in the law of the negation of the negation, what would count as a thesis and antithesis. And Engels was ambivalent as to the heuristic quality of the laws: sometimes he gave the impression that dialectical thinking was little more than the realization that there were no hard and fast lines of demarcation in nature. Yet at the same time he could talk of the 'proofs' of these laws (he seemed to mean 'examples') and describe the dialectic as 'a method of arriving at new results' or even of 'proving' as opposed to simply a very general (and some would say therefore almost superfluous) categorization of the results of natural science.

The story that Einstein, when confronted with the manuscripts of the *Dialectics of Nature*, insisted that they must at all costs be preserved as a fascinating resumé of all the misconceptions attendant on natural science at the end of the nineteenth century, is probably apocryphal. But it is difficult to believe that Engels' views contain much of lasting value either to science or to philosophy. However, as the basis for what came to be known as dialectical materialism, they were undoubtedly of immense influence.

5 Conclusion: Engels and Marx

To get a satisfactory picture of Engels, it is necessary to clarify as much as possible his relationship with Marx. Much that has been written about Marxism has given the impression that Engels and Marx were a sort of composite personality. Engels himself conveyed this impression by being unduly modest about his own role. 'All my life', he wrote in 1884, 'I have done what I was cut out for – namely to play second fiddle – and I think that I have done quite well in that capacity. And I have been happy to have had such a wonderful first violin as Marx.' Yet it is clear that Engels and Marx were very different in temperament and outlook. Moreover, Engels contributed enormously to Marx's achievement – not only financially and emotionally but also in terms of the genesis and evolution of his ideas.

In many respects it would be difficult to find two characters more opposed than those of Engels and Marx. Engels' clothes, for example, were always immaculate: he was invariably trim and scrupulously clean and described by Marx's son-in-law Lafargue as 'always looking as though ready to go on parade as during his years of voluntary service in the Prussian army'. Marx paid much less attention to washing and grooming, and was regarded by several of his acquaintances as a bohemian. Again, Engels was as methodical as an old maid, his study was like a dentist's reception room and all his books and papers were kept in an impeccable order; Marx's books were all over the place, often jumbled up with household articles.

Engels' handwriting was neat and clear; Marx's was notoriously illegible.

These differences extended to more fundamental matters. Marx – though he sometimes regretted it profoundly – was essentially a family man; engaged when he was only seventeen, he retained a lifelong attachment to his wife, who bore him seven children. By contrast, Engels remained unmarried; he was a great womanizer in his youth, and even in Manchester he lived a semi-bachelor existence despite his attachment to Mary Burns. This contrast in attitudes to domestic life was the source of the one note of discord in their friendship. Marx's wife disapproved of the relationship with Mary Burns and refused to meet her. When Mary died, Engels complained of Marx's 'frosty reception' of the news – though his own self-centred reaction was nothing to be proud of. He contrasted Marx's attitude with the sympathy of his 'philistine' acquaintances, and continued: 'You found the moment suitable to enforce the superiority of your cold thought processes.' Marx apologized and Engels replied that he was relieved not to have lost his friend and Mary Burns at the same time. Moreover, Marx's remarks on the death of Lizzie Burns do show him somewhat contemptuous of her illiteracy. That these may not have been isolated instances is suggested by the fact that on Marx's death his daughters destroyed a certain number of letters that might have given hurt to Engels.

Their different dispositions on family matters did, however, enable Engels to render a signal service to Marx: accepting temporary paternity of his illegitimate son Frederick Demuth. Indeed, Marx's debts to his friend were innumerable. Apart from affording him the one profound and stable friendship of his life, and all that that implied, Engels assisted him in a most material way.

During the late 1840s Marx had been comparatively well off, but soon after settling in London he was virtually destitute. During the last thirty years of his life, Marx lived off Engels. At first, Engels could only arrange relatively small amounts sent sometimes in stamps – or bank notes torn in half and mailed in separate envelopes for security reasons. From the late 1860s, however, Engels was able to settle a generous annual income on him. In terms of present-day values, Engels subsidized Marx and his family to the extent of over £100,000. More than that, Engels was always ready to put aside his own work in favour of Marx's: when Marx got an offer of a job as correspondent for the *New York Daily Tribune* but felt his English to be inadequate, Engels sent him regular articles that he could forward under his own name. When Marx turned to him for advice on military matters, agrarian economics, the latest progress in the natural sciences, or simply the practical workings of the capitalist system as exemplified in the firm of Ermen and Engels, his friend was always ready to supply the necessary information.

Engels also had a decisive influence on Marx's thinking. At a crucial point he directed Marx's attention towards what was to be his life's work, the study of economics – furnishing him with some of his basic concepts. For it was the article that Engels contributed to Marx's *Franco–German Annals* at the end of 1843 – his *Outline of a Critique of Political Economy* – that first aroused Marx's interest in the science of political economy. Fifteen years later Marx still described this article as 'a brilliant critical essay on economic categories'. In fact it sketched out many of the themes that were to become fundamental to Marxism: the factors governing economic growth, the phenomenon of the trade cycle, the contrast of growing wealth on the one side and growing impoverishment on the other, the polarization of classes and the tendency of open competition to give rise to monopoly. In the notebooks that constituted his famous *Economic and Philosophical Manuscripts of 1844*, the first work that Marx excerpted in the economics section was this article by Engels. It was largely due to this inspiration offered by Engels that, when he and Marx met in Paris in September of 1844, they found themselves 'in complete agreement on questions of theory'. The first works setting out the materialist conception of history – *The Holy Family*, *The German Ideology* and *The Communist Manifesto* – were all joint productions. This influence of Engels was consolidated by his *Condition of the Working Class* which continued, with a wealth of detail, many of the themes of the *Outlines*. His work, moreover, made pioneering use of the statistical material made available by the Registrar General, Factory Inspectors and parliamentary enquiries. This foreshadowed the impressive use which Marx made of such sources in the historical sections of *Capital*. Finally, the immense contribution of Engels in editing subsequent volumes of *Capital* should not be forgotten. This task absorbed his energies during the last twelve years of his life and no one but he could have produced volumes II and III as we have them today.

Engels summed up his relationship to Marx as follows:

I cannot deny that both before and during my forty years' partnership with Marx I had a certain independent share in working out the theory. But Marx was responsible for the leading basic ideas particularly as far as economics and history were concerned – and he put those ideas in their final classic form. What I achieved – apart from work in a few specialized fields of study – Marx could have achieved without me. But what Marx achieved I could not have achieved.

There are two main reasons why this is somewhat too modest. The first (as detailed above) is that Engels did have a decisive influence on Marx at the beginning of his career. The second is that Engels' views always did have a slightly different emphasis and that this came to the fore particularly after Marx's death, when Engels established an interpretation of 'Marxism' somewhat divergent from Marx's own ideas. It has been said that the latest post-humous service that Engels still renders his friend is to take the blame for those bits of Marxist thought which some modern Marxists cannot or do not want to defend. It would obviously be unacceptable to suggest that there was *no* continuity between Marx's work and the views of the later Engels. But, equally, the divergences are there — and they go back a long way.

The background and education of Engels and Marx were very different and must have had some influence on the later development of their thought. Engels had a very strong Pietist upbringing and had a hard struggle to free himself from his religious beliefs; thus his materialist views tended to be more pronounced and more polemical than those of Marx, who never seems to have been at all attracted by religion. Again, Engels was an autodidact who, while earning a living in business or the army, picked up his views in his spare time and moved very rapidly towards his researches on economics and the working class. In particular, he never went through the profound, systematic, full-time wrestling with Hegel that Marx engaged in for seven arduous years before his espousal of communism. These differences tended to be reinforced by the unofficial division of labour between Engels and Marx in their collective enterprise. Marx devoted himself to political economy, whereas Engels concentrated on military history and, more particularly, the natural sciences. Moreover, where Marx concentrated on investigating the more fundamental aspects of the materialist conception of history, Engels was saddled with the task of defending their views in public – a task which almost of necessity involved oversimplification.

The result of these differing backgrounds and pre-occupations is clearly shown by comparing Engels' *Principles of Communism* with the final draft of *The Communist Manifesto* for which Marx alone was responsible. Marx, from his background of Hegel, Young Hegelianism and French socialism, put emphasis on politics, on consciousness and on class struggle: Engels, impressed by English political economy, spoke more of the economic consequences of technological growth and the Industrial Revolution. Marx's treatment involved dialectical transitions which seemed to owe something to Hegel: Engels had a concept of development that was determined by technology and owed more to the Enlightenment.

These differences were also apparent in their views of historical development and the nature of communism: whereas Marx came to see a multilinear development out of communal peasant society, Engels – particularly in his *Origin* – saw only a unilinear path of development. But this divergence is at its most striking in their picture of communist society. Engels' picture in *Anti-Dühring* is simple and optimistic. Once the means of production have been seized by society, then

men's social organization which had hitherto stood in opposition to them as if arbitrarily decreed by nature and history, will become the voluntary act of men themselves.

The objective, external forces which have hitherto dominated history, will then pass under the control of men themselves. It is only from this point that men, with full consciousness, will fashion their own history; it is only from this point that the social causes set in motion by men will have, in predominantly increasing measure, the effects willed by men. It is humanity's leap from the realm of necessity into the realm of freedom.

Marx, by contrast, wrote in a well-known passage of *Capital* that in the realm of productive labour

> freedom can only consist in socialized men, the associated producers, rationally regulating their interchange with nature, bringing it under their common control, instead of being ruled by it as by the blind forces of nature; and achieving this with the least expenditure of energy and under conditions most favourable to, and worthy of, their human nature. But it nonetheless still remains a realm of necessity. Beyond it begins that development of human energy which is an end in itself, the true realm of freedom which, however, can blossom forth only with this realm of necessity as its basis.

The contrast between the two passages is marked. Marx is less optimistic and more dialectical than Engels: necessity cannot be abolished but must be used as an ineradicable basis.

This difference in attitude to the final form of human history is paralleled by the divergence of Marx and Engels on its beginnings. It was Engels' acceptance of Morgan's views of the evolution of sexual relationships (the least tenable part of his work) that led him to adopt a Darwinian schema and interpret the dynamic of primitive society differently from that of later history. Marx paid much less attention to this area and centred his interests on the clan system. It was inside this economico-political framework that he considered the social position of women : Engels, by contrast, considered the various forms of promiscuity to be paramount. In general, Engels tended to contrast present society both with primitive communism and with future communism and to some extent saw an idealized communism in the past as a model for the communism to come. In this he followed Rousseau. Marx, however, made no such parallels and understood primitive communism in terms of contemporary society, itself viewed as a dialectical process giving birth to future communism. In this he followed Hegel.

Engels' contribution to the legacy of Marx culminated in the decisive role that he played in the tendency to transform Marx's views into a *Weltanschauung*, a philosophical system, an interpretation of the world. Both the huge growth of numbers in the Marxist Social Democratic Party, and the increasing prestige of the natural sciences as holding the key to human progress, served to facilitate this process. The growth in the number of adherents required a systematic doctrine that was easily understandable, and the prestige of the scientific outlook meant that it had to be couched in similar terms, for the average member of the SPD was already strongly influenced by vulgar-materialist accounts of the world. Engels' gifts as a quick and lucid writer – a vulgarizer in the best sense of the word – admirably fitted him for the role of doctrinal mentor for the emergent Marxist movement. Already in his speech at Marx's graveside, he had declared : 'Just as Darwin discovered the law of development of organic nature, so Marx discovered the law of development of human history.'

Thus began the gradual assimilation of Marx's views to a scientific world outlook : of course Marx himself called his work scientific (so did Hegel), but in his work the term had much less the connotation of natural scientific methodology. It was mainly with Engels and his successors that the notion of 'scientific socialism' became narrowed and progressively emasculated. It is significant in this context that the concept of 'matter' of which Engels made such constant use in *Anti-Dühring* and the *Dialectics of Nature* was entirely foreign to Marx's work. The laws of the dialectic were said by Engels to be operative in a nature that existed objectively and independent of the human mind. Thus the world of nature and the world of history fell apart in two separate fields of study – whereas for Marx one of the central aspects of the dialectic consisted precisely in the interaction of man and his surroundings. For Marx, any attempt to construct a sort of objective basis for a study of the historical process outside that process itself was doomed to failure : for all thought was social and its significance would only be grasped through a study of society.

A specific illustration of this difference is the attitude of Marx and Engels to Feuerbach. Whereas Marx had criticised Feuerbach for not understanding materialism in a *historical* way and therefore not viewing man's history as being conditioned by his material needs, Engels attacked Feuerbach because he did not comprehend 'the universe as a process of matter undergoing uninterrupted historical development' and was therefore 'idealist'. The very readiness of Engels to devote himself to a relatively lengthy study of Feuerbach (like his own disciple Plekhanov) is also symptomatic of his interest in materialism as a philosophical interpretation of the world.

Although Engels naturally cannot be saddled with the sole responsibility for the evolution of Marxist doctrine, it was to his authority that subsequent Marxists often appealed – especially in the realm of philosophy. Marxism became progressively equated with dialectical materialism – an expression totally absent not only from Marx but also from Engels (it was first used by Dietzgen during the 1870s and popularized by Lenin's teacher Plekhanov, who leant heavily on Engels). For on specifically philosophical questions, the leading theoreticians of the Second International, with Kautsky at their head, were strongly influenced by Engels. Indeed, many of them had been led to Marxism by the reading of *Anti-Dühring*. In Russia, too, Lenin's book on *Materialism and Empirio-Criticism* set a similar tone. This work (unlike his subsequent *Philosophical Notebooks*) was more to be valued for its political purpose – to prevent the Bolsheviks being attacked for unorthodoxy in philosophy – rather than for its philosophical value, which is very low. Lenin relied almost exclusively on quotations from Engels; Marx was notably absent. Crude materialism is the most conservative of doctrines and it is not surprising that, with the consolidation of the Stalinist regime, the vulgarizations of Engels should have become the main philosophical content of Soviet textbooks – a situation that is not much changed today.

The reaction was inevitable: one of the first and most influential contributors was George Lukács who, in his *History and Class Consciousness* (1921), proposed a very Hegelian reading of Marx, which contrasted sharply with Engels' version. And he was followed almost simultaneously by Karl Korsch with his *Marxism and Philosophy*. More decisively, the publication in the early 1930s of Marx's early and more humanist writings helped to give a different emphasis to western Marxism and produced a reaction against Engels' philosophical formulations, which tended to be associated almost exclusively with Stalinist dogmatism. Indeed, to most Marxist activists the question of the existence of a dialectic in nature (as opposed to a dialectic in society) seemed to be a quasi-metaphysical problem very far removed from pressing political and social concerns. And this reaction has only partly been mitigated by the more recent interest in structuralist versions of Marxism and in questions of Marx's methodology.

Yet these considerations should in no way diminish our appreciation of the immense contributions of Engels to the socialist movement. Marx wrote of his friend that he was 'a real encyclopaedia, ready for work at every hour of the day or night, quick to write and busy as the devil'. It is indeed the universality of Engels' contribution that is striking. Although lacking, as he himself was the first to admit, the towering genius of Marx, Engels exploited his immense talents in the most varied directions; he was a first-rate linguist, a distinguished military critic, at least the equal of Marx as a historian, a pioneer in anthropology, and the acknowledged mentor of a dozen emergent Marxist parties. Engels perhaps drew more than Marx on the intellectual legacy of the eighteenth-century Enlightenment, and his very universality puts one in mind of an eighteenth-century *philosophe*. He also possessed the unquenchable optimism of the Enlightenment and preserved to the end his belief in the imminence of a truly proletarian revolution – a belief that would with difficulty have survived far into the more troubled twentieth century.

Further Reading

Engels – unlike many other Marxists – is easy to read, having a clear style with a minimum of jargon. This is possibly the reason why there are fewer commentaries on him than on almost any other major socialist thinker. All the more reason, therefore, for going directly to the originals.

1 COMPLETE WORKS

There is a complete edition of the works of Marx and Engels in English in progress, published by Lawrence and Wishart in London and International Publishers in New York. In all, it will amount to some fifty volumes. To date, the volumes up to the end of the 1840s have been published; completion will take a further ten years.

2 SELECTIONS

The only selection of Engels' work in English is *Engels*, ed. W. O. Henderson, Harmondsworth 1967. There are several selections of Marx and Engels' works together. Perhaps the most accessible is: Karl Marx, Frederick Engels, *Selected Works*, Moscow 1935 (several reprints). This selection has the advantage of reproducing excerpts *in extenso*, including the whole of the *Origin* and *Ludwig Feuerbach* and a substantial extract from *Anti-Dühring*. Lesser extracts are contained in: Marx and Engels, *Basic Writings on Politics and Philosophy*, ed. L. Feuer, New York 1959, and *The Marx–Engels Reader*, ed. R. Tucker, New York 1972. There are also numerous selections, published by Moscow, of Marx and Engels *On Religion*, *On Ireland*, *On Britain*, *On Literature and Art* etc.

3 INDIVIDUAL WORKS
Anti-Dühring, Ludwig Feuerbach, Dialectics of Nature, Origin, have been translated in separate editions by Lawrence and Wishart and International Publishers, the latter with a substantial introduction by Eleanor Leacock. Engels' articles on the German Revolution of 1848–9 have been edited by Eleanor Marx: *Revolution and Counter-Revolution in Germany in 1848*, London 1971, as also Engels' writings on military matters: *Engels as Military Critic*, ed. W. Henderson and O. Chaloner, London 1959. The same editors produced a new translation and edition of *The Condition of the Working Class in England*, Oxford 1958. The commentary of this edition is very critical of Engels. For the other side, see the Panther edition with an introduction by E. Hobsbawm, St Albans 1969.

4 COMMENTARIES
There is a commentary on Engels' *The Condition of the Working Class in England* from a literary and psychological point of view by S. Marcus, *Engels, Manchester, and the Working Class*, New York 1974. Of biographies, there is the abridged Gustav Mayer, *Friedrich Engels*, London 1936, which is but a pale shadow of Mayer's splendid two-volume biography in German, which is the best so far available. Grace Carlton's *Friedrich Engels: The Shadow Prophet*, London 1965, is rather thin. The Russian biography in English, *Frederick Engels: a biography*, Moscow 1974, contains a lot of details – but is also an extreme example of hagiography. The same is true of the East German *Frederick Engels: a biography*, Dresden 1972. Recently there has appeared W. O. Henderson's *The Life of Friedrich Engels*, two volumes, London 1976. This is strong on the personal side and also on the factual historical, but is uniformly unsympathetic to Engels and has virtually no assessment of him as a theorist. For the personal side of Engels' later years, see also: Y. Kapp, *Eleanor Marx: The Crowded Years*, London 1976. Gareth Stedman Jones will be producing a full-length study of Engels in about four years' time.

Chronology

1820   Birth in Barmen
1835–7   High School in Elberfeld
1837–8   Work in father's firm, Barmen
1838–41   Clerical work in Bremen
1841–2   Military service in Berlin
1842   November: first meeting with Marx
1842–4   Work in father's firm: Manchester
1844   Beginning of collaboration with Marx
      Outlines of a Critique of Political Economy
1845   Moves to Brussels
      The Condition of the Working Class in England
1846   *The German Ideology*
1847   Communist League activities in Paris and London
1848   Work on *Neue Rheinische Zeitung* in Cologne
1849   Collapse of revolution
      Military campaign in south Germany
      Sails to London
1850   Moves to Manchester to work in Ermen and Engels
1851   Begins writing for *New York Daily Tribune*
1860   Death of father
1863   Death of Mary Burns
1869   Leaves Ermen and Engels
1870   Moves back to London
1870–2   Work for First International
1873   Death of Engels' mother
1873–8   Work on *Dialectics of Nature*
1877–8   *Anti-Dühring*
1878   Death of Lizzie Burns
1883   Death of Marx
1884   *The Origin of the Family, Private Property and the State*

1885 Volume II of *Capital*
1893 President of Zürich Congress of Second International
1894 Volume III of *Capital*
1895 Preface to Marx's *Class Struggles in France*
       Death of Engels

Fontana Modern Masters

General Editor: Frank Kermode

ARTAUD	*Martin Esslin*
BECKETT	*A. Alvarez*
CAMUS	*Conor Cruise O'Brien*
CHOMSKY	*John Lyons*
EINSTEIN	*Jeremy Bernstein*
ELIOT	*Stephen Spender*
ENGELS	*David McLellan*
FANON	*David Caute*
FREUD	*Richard Wollheim*
GANDHI	*George Woodcock*
GRAMSCI	*James Joll*
JOYCE	*John Gross*
JUNG	*Anthony Storr*
KAFKA	*Erich Heller*
KEYNES	*D. E. Moggridge*
LAWRENCE	*Frank Kermode*
LAING	*E. Z. Friedenberg*
LE CORBUSIER	*Stephen Gardiner*
LENIN	*Robert Conquest*
LEVI-STRAUSS	*Edmund Leach*
MARCUSE	*Alasdair MacIntyre*
MARX	*David McLellan*
ORWELL	*Raymond Williams*
POPPER	*Brian Magee*
POUND	*Donald Davie*
PROUST	*Roger Shattuck*
REICH	*Charles Rycroft*
RUSSELL	*A. J. Ayer*
SARTRE	*Arthur C. Danto*
SAUSSURE	*Jonathan Culler*
SCHOENBERG	*Charles Rosen*
WEBER	*Donald MacRae*
WITTGENSTEIN	*David Pears*
YEATS	*Denis Donoghue*